Let's Celebrate Freedom!

THE DECLARATION OF INDEPENDENCE

Lorijo Metz

PowerKiDS
press

New York

Dedicated to my father, Joe Rush, who taught me the importance of history

Published in 2014 by The Rosen Publishing Group, Inc.
29 East 21st Street, New York, NY 10010

First Edition

Editor: Amelie von Zumbusch
Book Design: Colleen Bialecki
Photo Research: Katie Stryker

Photo Credits: Cover SuperStock/Getty Images; p. 4 Photos.com/Thinkstock; p. 5 Gary718/Shutterstock.com; pp. 7, 12 MPI/Stringer/Archive Photos/Getty Images; p. 9 trekandshoot/Shutterstock.com; pp. 11, 13 (bottom) John Parrot/Stock Trek Images/Getty Images; p. 12 Culture Club/Contributor/Hulton Archive/Getty Images; p. 13 (top) MPI/Stringer/Archive Photos/Getty Images p. 14 FPG/Taxi/Getty Images; p. 15 Universal Images Group/Getty Images; p. 16 Tetra Images/Getty Images; p. 17 Victorian Traditions/Shutterstock.com; p. 18 Allan Ramsay/The Bridgeman Art Library/Getty Images; p. 19 US Army Center of Military History; p. 20 Library of Congress Prints and Photographs Division Washington, D.C.; p. 21 Stringer/AFP/Getty Images; p. 22 Hiroyuki Matsumoto/Stone/Getty Images.

Library of Congress Cataloging-in-Publication Data

Metz, Lorijo.
The Declaration of Independence / by Lorijo Metz. — First Edition.
    pages cm. — (Let's celebrate freedom!)
Includes index.
ISBN 978-1-4777-2894-9 (library) — ISBN 978-1-4777-2983-0 (pbk.) —
ISBN 978-1-4777-3053-9 (6-pack)
1. United States. Declaration of Independence—Juvenile literature. 2. United States—Politics and government—1775–1783—Juvenile literature. I. Title.
E221.M48 2014
973.3′13—dc23
                                    2013022315

Manufactured in the United States of America

CPSIA Compliance Information: Batch # W14PK4: For Further Information contact Rosen Publishing, New York, New York at 1-800-237-9932

CONTENTS

HAPPY BIRTHDAY, AMERICA!

Every year, on July 4, Americans celebrate **Independence** Day. Another word for "independence" is "freedom." In 1776, the people of America's original 13 **colonies** were not yet free. King George III of Great Britain ruled them. He had passed many unfair laws, and fighting had broken out between American and British troops.

Thomas Jefferson was one of the delegates who met in Philadelphia in 1776. He represented, or spoke for, Virginia.

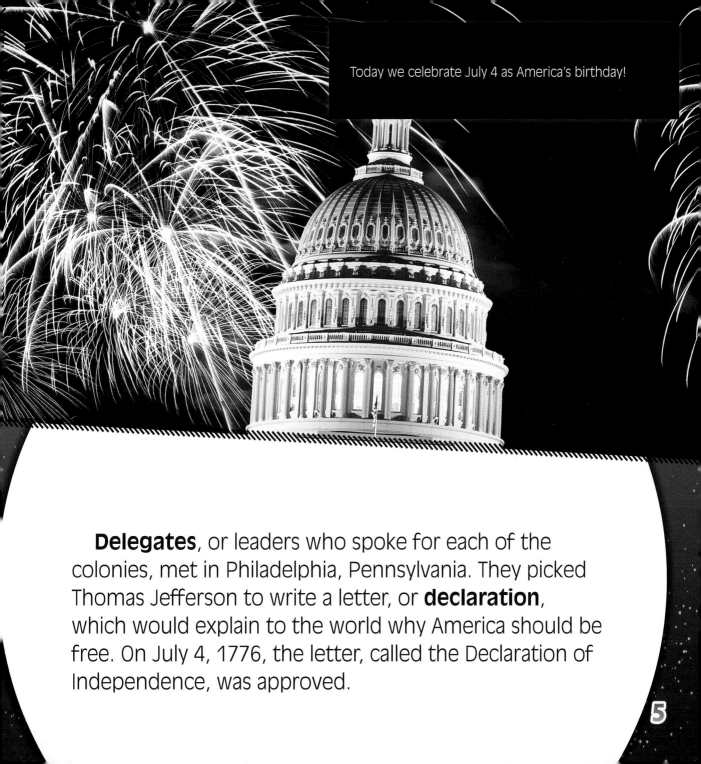

Today we celebrate July 4 as America's birthday!

Delegates, or leaders who spoke for each of the colonies, met in Philadelphia, Pennsylvania. They picked Thomas Jefferson to write a letter, or **declaration**, which would explain to the world why America should be free. On July 4, 1776, the letter, called the Declaration of Independence, was approved.

In 1763, Britain won a war to keep France out of North America. This war, called the French and Indian War, was expensive. To raise money, the British **Parliament**, or government, began taxing the colonists. They taxed items like sugar, coffee, and books. Some colonists believed that the taxes were unfair because the colonists had no **representation**, or people to speak for them, in Parliament.

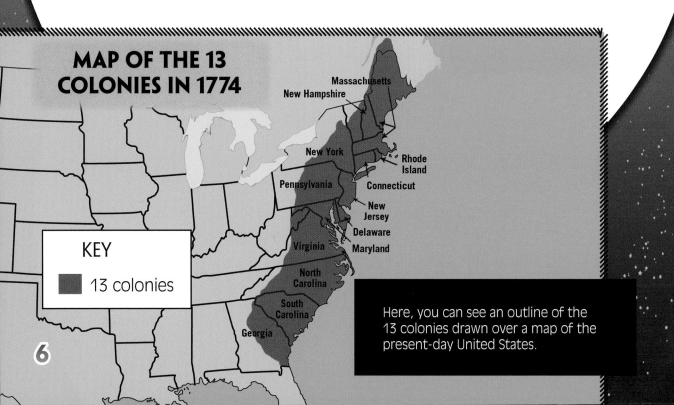

MAP OF THE 13 COLONIES IN 1774

Massachusetts
New Hampshire
New York
Rhode Island
Pennsylvania
Connecticut
New Jersey
Delaware
Virginia
Maryland
North Carolina
South Carolina
Georgia

KEY
■ 13 colonies

Here, you can see an outline of the 13 colonies drawn over a map of the present-day United States.

Some colonists dressed as Native Americans to disguise themselves during the Boston Tea Party.

On April 27, 1773, Parliament passed a tax on tea. That December, colonists **rebelled**, or fought back, by throwing hundreds of chests of British tea into the harbor in Boston, Massachusetts. This rebellion became known as the Boston Tea Party.

On April 18, 1775, Paul Revere made his famous midnight ride from Boston to Lexington, Massachusetts. He rode to warn fellow colonists that British troops were coming to take their weapons. The next day, as British troops marched through Lexington on their way to Concord, shooting broke out between the troops and the colonists. The American Revolution had begun!

That May, delegates from the colonies gathered in Philadelphia for the Second Continental Congress. They appointed George Washington as the leader of the newly formed Continental army. The delegates sent one final appeal to Great Britain's King George III, but he refused to listen.

The Second Continental Congress met in the Pennsylvania statehouse. The building is now known as Independence Hall.

On June 7, 1776, Richard Henry Lee of Virginia presented a bold **resolution**, or proposal, to the members of the Second Continental Congress. It said that the 13 colonies should be "free and independent states." At that point, the delegates did not all think that the colonies should separate from England.

Five men, including Benjamin Franklin, John Adams, and Thomas Jefferson, were asked to write a declaration that would explain why America should be free. The group picked Jefferson, a talented writer, to be the declaration's main author. After much **debate**, Lee's resolution was passed on July 2. On July 4, 1776, the leaders adopted the Declaration of Independence!

This painting shows Jefferson and the other members of the Committee of Five presenting the Declaration of Independence to the Second Continental Congress.

February 10, 1763

The Treaty of Paris is signed, ending the French and Indian War.

June 29, 1767

Parliament passes the Townshend Acts, taxing paint, glass, and other goods from Britain.

1760 1762 1764 1766 1768 1770

March 22, 1765

Parliament passes the Stamp Act, taxing all printed paper goods.

December 16, 1773

The Boston Tea Party takes place.

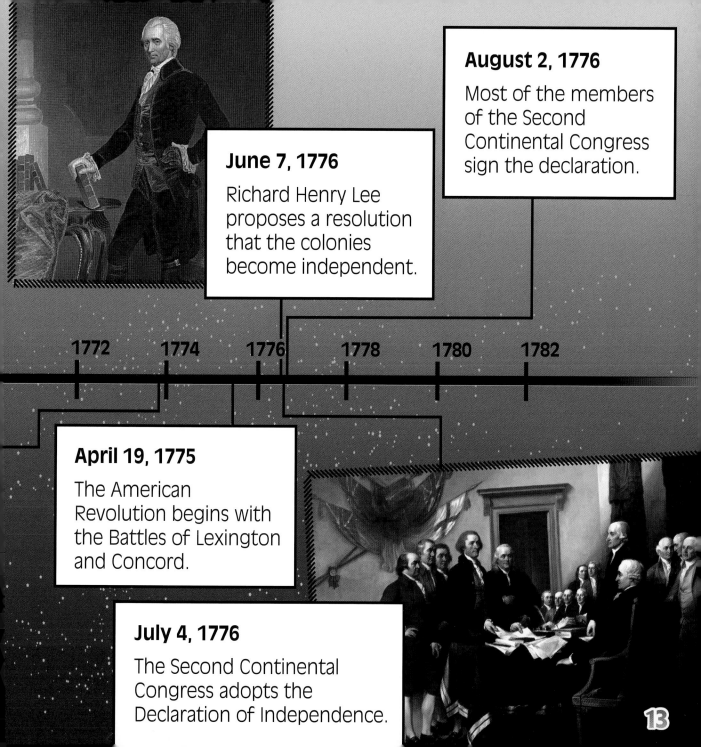

August 2, 1776

Most of the members of the Second Continental Congress sign the declaration.

June 7, 1776

Richard Henry Lee proposes a resolution that the colonies become independent.

1772 1774 1776 1778 1780 1782

April 19, 1775

The American Revolution begins with the Battles of Lexington and Concord.

July 4, 1776

The Second Continental Congress adopts the Declaration of Independence.

13

Declaring independence from a nation as powerful as Great Britain was a brave act. In 1776, America was just 13 small colonies. However, the Declaration of Independence was aimed at a big audience. It explained the colonists' reasons for seeking independence to the king and the British people.

John Hancock is famous for being the first to sign the Declaration of Independence. The signers took a big risk, as they knew that the British would consider their actions treason.

This image shows the Declaration of Independence being read aloud in New York City on July 9, 1776. At the time, Washington and most of the Continental army were based there.

It was also adressed to the rest of the world, in the hopes of gaining support for the colonists' cause. Perhaps most importantly, the declaration was written for the colonists. There were public readings of it in many cities. For example, George Washington had it read to his troops in New York City.

One of the most famous lines in the Declaration of Independence is found near the beginning. It reads, "We hold these truths to be self-evident, that all men are created equal, that they are endowed by their Creator with certain unalienable Rights, that among these are Life, Liberty, and the pursuit of Happiness— That to secure these Rights, Governments are instituted among Men, deriving their just powers from the consent of the governed."

Today, Americans can show whether or not they agree with the actions of the government by voting.

Franklin and Adams suggested changes to help Jefferson come up with the final wording for the declaration before it was presented to Congress.

In other words, everyone is created equal, with certain rights that cannot be taken away. To protect those rights, governments are created. Their power and the right to govern, however, come from the people they serve.

The declaration explains, "Governments long established should not be changed for light and transient causes." This means that people should have very good reasons for leaving one government to start another. To prove the colonists had good reasons, the declaration goes on to include a list of **grievances**, or complaints, against the king of England.

This is George III of Great Britain. The declaration argues that "the history of the present King of Great Britain is a history of repeated injuries."

One of the grievances listed in the declaration is that the British hired Hessian soldiers to help fight the war. These soldiers took part in the Battle of Trenton, seen here.

For example, the king would not let the colonists pass necessary laws without his approval. He fired leaders who did not agree with him. He also made the colonists house and feed British soldiers. In all, the declaration lists 27 grievances against George III.

INSPIRING CHANGE

The Declaration of Independence declares that "all men are created equal." However, not all Americans had equal rights in 1776. For example, many African Americans were slaves. Even those that were free had fewer rights than white Americans. Women's rights were limited, too.

In 1861, President Abraham Lincoln said, "I have never had a feeling politically that did not spring from the sentiments embodied in the Declaration of Independence."

King gave his "I Have a Dream" speech at a protest called the March on Washington. It took place on August 28, 1963.

Over the years, the declaration has **inspired** many Americans to fight for equality. In 1848, the Declaration of Sentiments from the women's rights convention in Seneca Falls, New York, stated that "all men and women are created equal." Civil rights leader Martin Luther King Jr. included the words "all men are created equal" in his famous "I Have a Dream" speech.

Today, you can see the original Declaration of Independence at the Rotunda of the National **Archives** Building, in Washington, DC. You can see the US Constitution and the Bill of Rights there, too. These are the **documents** on which American freedoms are built. As a group, the three are called the Charters of Freedom.

The Declaration of Independence continues to inspire thoughts of freedom and equality. Have you ever heard people quote its famous words?

These people are looking at the original Declaration of Independence at the National Archives. The declaration has been kept there since 1952.

GLOSSARY

archives (AR-kyvz) A place where records or historical documents are kept.

colonies (KAH-luh-neez) New places where people move that are still ruled by the leaders of the countries from which they came.

debate (dih-BAYT) Argument.

declaration (deh-kluh-RAY-shun) An official announcement of something.

delegates (DEH-lih-gets) People acting for another person or a group of people.

documents (DOK-yoo-ments) Written or printed statements that give official information about something.

grievances (GREE-vints-ez) Complaints about practices that one believes to be wrong.

independence (in-dih-PEN-dents) Freedom from the control of other people.

inspired (in-SPY-urd) Moved someone to do something.

Parliament (PAR-leh-ment) The group in Great Britain that makes the country's laws.

rebelled (rih-BELD) Disobeyed the people or country in charge.

representation (reh-prih-zen-TAY-shun) Acting in the place of or for someone else, usually by legal right.

resolution (reh-zuh-LOO-shun) A formal statement adopted by a group of people.

INDEX

WEBSITES

Due to the changing nature of Internet links, PowerKids Press has developed an online list of websites related to the subject of this book. This site is updated regularly. Please use this link to access the list: www.powerkidslinks.com/lcf/declar/